CLASSIFIED INTELLIGENCE

THE MIRACLE OF NIKOLA TESLA'S PURPLE ENERGY PLATES

TIM R. SWARTZ
AND
TIMOTHY GREEN BECKLEY

Classified Intelligence Report On . . .

THE MIRACLE
OF
NIKOLA TESLA'S
PURPLE ENERGY PLATES

By Tim R. Swartz
and
Timothy Green Beckley

Inner Light Publications/Global Communications

The Miracle of Nikola Tesla's Purple Energy Plates

Timothy Green Beckley: Editorial Director

Carol Ann Rodriguez: Publishers Assistant
Editor & Layout: Tim R. Swartz
Sean Casteel: Associate Editor
William Kern: Associate Editor & Art Consultant

Email: mrufo8@hotmail.com

Conspiracyjournal.com

www.teslasecretlab.com

CONTENTS

TESLA'S "LOST" INVENTIONS AND THE SECRET OF THE PURPLE HARMONY PLATES

I recently was asked by The History Channel to be a part of the new, six-part series *"The Tesla Files."* I was flown to Washington DC and spent several days filming along with hosts astrophysicist Travis Taylor and investigative journalist Jason Stapleton. We discussed in length the declassified FBI files concerning Nikola Tesla and what may have happened to his papers, notes and journals that vanished after he died in 1943. In these FBI files, there is mention of Ralph Bergstresser, a friend of Tesla's who reported to the FBI his concern that foreign agents may have targeted Tesla to steal his notes and inventions, or possibly even kidnap him. Bergstresser is significant to his connection with Nikola Tesla because Bergstresser is the inventor of the Tesla Purple Harmony (or Energy) Plates. This booklet examines the history of this incredible invention, how they work, and personal testimonies from satisfied people that have used them.

- Tim R. Swartz, author of "The Lost Journals of Nikola Tesla"

When asked who he felt was the world's greatest inventor, science editor and publisher, Hugo Gemsback, said. "If you mean the man who really invented, in other words, originated and discovered - not merely improved what had already been invented by others - then without a shade of doubt Nikola Tesla is the world's greatest inventor, not only at present but in all history..."

Indeed, Nikola Tesla is probably the greatest genius the world has never known. Born on July 9, 1856 in Smiljan, Lika, Croatia, Tesla came to the United States and created new technologies that led to such scientific marvels as the AC motor, radio, fluorescent lights, radar, diathermy, the high-frequency furnace, wave-guide for microwave transmission, space navigation code, cryogenic engineering, electrotherapeutics, energy transmission to satellites, principles of solid state transistor technology and the reciprocating dynamo to name only a few.

In his younger years, Tesla sensed the universe was: "Composed of a symphony of alternating currents with the harmonies played on a vast range of octaves. The 60-cycles-per-second AC was but a single note in a lower octave. In one of the higher octaves at a frequency of billions of cycles per second was visible light."

To explore this whole range of electrical vibration between his low-frequency alternating current and light waves, he sensed, would bring him closer to an understanding of the cosmic symphony. Tesla's genius with electricity received further stimulation through his interest in resonance. The ubiquitous Tesla Coil is evidence of the synergy of electricity and vibrations with a power cord from an insulated handle at one end and primary and secondary coils tuned to resonate at the other end. The Tesla Coil, when plugged in, begins to vibrate and hum. The small Tesla Coil generates high voltages and high frequencies and is used in one form or another in every radio and television set and can be found in every university science laboratory.

It has been said that resonance is a manner in which nature works. It covers all aspects of science from electricity to nuclear fusion. Nothing exists in the Universe that does not have vibration. Nikola knew that vibration is the rapid back-and-forth motion of an object, which creates waves. He also knew that resonance is the effect of these waves on another object when, in 1898, he made an oscillator no larger than a fist and attached it to a steel link two feet long and two inches thick.

"For a long time nothing happened..." he said. "But at last, the great steel link began to tremble, increased its trembling until it dilated and contracted like a beating heart - and finally broke!"

In his later years, Tesla believed that all matter came from a primary substance, the luminiferous ether, which filled all space. He said in 1942: "If you want to find the secrets of the Universe, think in terms of energy, frequency and vibration. The Universe is energy and each basic element of the known atomic chart consists of energy at different rates of vibration. The difference between any two elements is the difference in both atomic structure and vibration rates."

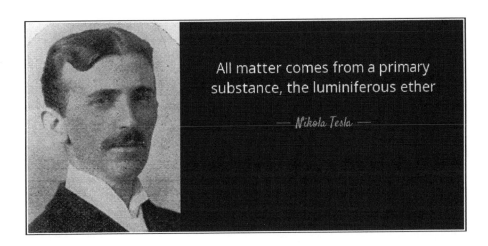

All matter comes from a primary substance, the luminiferous ether

— Nikola Tesla —

The Creation of the Purple Energy Plates

In 1943, another young electrical engineer named Ralph Bergstresser met Tesla in a combined effort to explore energetic options to help end World War II. Bergstresser was impressed with the knowledge, demeanor and deep abiding humanitarian ideals of Tesla. Tesla gave Ralph inspiration regarding his knowledge and access of "free energy" when he offered Ralph a curious clue: "If you want to understand the secrets of nature, look to vibration and frequency."

Tesla died two months after his meeting with Ralph. Although he lamented the passing of such a great light, Bergstresser was exhilarated by the possibilities and potential of free energy. With this, the torch of enlightenment had been passed on. Bergstresser soon blended the futuristic thoughts about frequency and his scientific expertise to serve humanity. Ralph Bergstresser spent the next 20-years of his life committed to breaking through the veil of matter to access free energy. He succeeded in doing this in the early 1960s.

Ralph was mindful of the oppression and ridicule Tesla had endured because he chose high ideals. Bergstresser decided on a different strategy in an attempt to get the free energy to the masses.

Bergstresser introduced the Tesla Purple Energy Plate to the world and chose an inexpensive medium (anodized aluminum) that, when altered, would act as a transceiver, a transceiver that drew in and radiated out Universal Life Force energy or "free energy." The plate enhanced and benefitted anyone or anything that was in close proximity to it. The plate was not charged like a battery, so it could never be discharged. As a matter of fact the original plates are still doing a fine job.

The Tesla Purple Energy Plates are a beautiful violet color and are a window into the 4th and 5th dimensional energy fields. They radiate life force energy (Chi/prana) for a distance of 10"-18". In no way can these plates be harmful.

Ralph Bergstresser says that there is a frequency or vibration of energy that fills the Universe. This energy is not only beneficial, but also essential to all living cells whether human, plant or animal. Man utilizes this energy with his mind. Every thought is transmitted by this energy. Every aspect of life in the physical depends on this basic energy or power of the Universe.

Spiritual growth is our only purpose and reason for being alive on earth. Each individual must learn how to utilize this energy for spiritual growth and constructive purposes. Constructive use (positive use) of this energy raises the level of consciousness of man and in turn raises his vibration rate or frequency.

Every individual has a different rate of vibration. All of man's earthly problems are created by his thought projections. What we project from our mind in the form of thoughts, we create and receive. Spiritual growth requires the elimination of all negative thought, which dissipates "the life force or vital energy."

Every individual, knowingly or otherwise, makes use of this energy. Our bodies use this energy to heal injuries, to reduce stress and fatigue, and to grow both physically and spiritually.

Without exception everyone has the ability to attract as much of this Universal energy as the individual s body and mind require. Unfortunately the seemingly hectic pace of modern life has most of us looking after day to day cares with precious little time to concentrate on attracting sufficient quantities of the vital Universal energy to meet our needs.

How Do Tesla Purple Energy Plates Work?

The atomic structure of Purple Plates has been altered, allowing the atoms and electrons e aluminum to resonate in tune with the basic energy that causes the particles of every atom and molecule to be m constant vibration. Once the structure of the atoms of the aluminum has been altered, they will remain in that condition, possibly indefinitely.

The plates create a positive energy field around themselves that will penetrate any material substance by osmosis. This energy is said to be beneficial to all life...plant, animal or human. Science has proven that by projecting love or positive energy to a plant, the plant will flourish. The plate energy will also do the same thing to plants.

Bums, cuts, aches and pains involve a sudden change to the normal vibration rate of tissue. The theory is that the energy around the plates helps to accelerate the healing and thus return the injured area to its normal rate of vibration.

Among the plates many uses are that they are worn to raise personal energy levels and to protect one against electromagnetic radiation (EMR) in the environment and from EMR-producing equipment, such as computers, televisions, etc. The life-force energy of the plates can be measured by radionic equipment.

When using this measurement, the energy level of an individual who has begun to work on him/herself might oscillate (or vibrate) around 25,000 cycles a second.

When this person holds a purple plate, the reading immediately increases to 90,000- 95.000 cycles a second. It will not remain at that level but with continual use of the plate, it will slowly increase to a steady 100,000 cycles per second. All faith healing utilizes this higher energy.

In his book "*Beyond Ascension - How To Complete The Seven Levels Of Initiation*," Joshua Stone refers to the plates: "One of the most extraordinary tools I have found to raise my overall energy and even light my quotient is the Positive Energy Plate. I am not one for gadgets. I have seen them all and I use almost none of them. The one exception I make is the use of the purple plate, which I am sure many of you have seen. It is actually a free-energy plate. The Purple Plate not only cleared the food of all negative energy and negative residues such as pesticides, but also energized the food. Now I put all my food on it and I continue to be amazed."

Many people use the large plates in their refrigerators to enhance flavor and freshness. By placing a glass of water on a small purple plate for approximately five minutes, you induce the high spiritual vibration of the seventh color ray (violet) Violet is also the color of the flame of Saint Germain, and corresponds with the 7th energy center in our bodies, also known as the crown chakra.

Some people sleep with a plate beneath their pillow to ensure restfulness, even when one has only slept a short time. Others cannot sleep with the plates nearby, as they will remain awake. Wearing a small plate will cause most people to feel an increase in energy. Others find the best results wearing them for shorter periods of time, perhaps 30 minutes or an hour each day.

Such energy takes different forms. For instance, scientific research tends to support what a great many gardeners already know: that projecting the positive energy of loving thoughts can make plants thrive more vigorously than usual. Another example of positive energy takes place when a mother lays her hands on a child's injury.

Some devotees of Yoga call this prana, a release of energy, and the pain is relieved. A great many users of the Purple Plates are emphatic that the plates can do the same thing when placed on an injured area of a person, plant, or animal. Most wear them all the time to raise personal energy levels and protect against electromagnetic radiation (EMR) in the environment and from EMR-producing equipment, e.g. computers, TVs, etc.

They point out that injuries, a bum for example, involves a sudden change to the normal vibration rate of tissue - with accompanying pain. The theory is that the plates help to quickly return the injured area to its normal rate of vibration, so relieving the pain. Users report that when the plates are placed upon bums, cuts, aches and pains in the human body, healing appears to be accelerated, and the pain lessens or disappears.

The Universal Energy of Vibrations is at the very foundation of physical existence, and through scientific innovation, millions of users worldwide are experiencing the help made available through the concentration of this "life force energy."

Many people doubt that the Tesla Purple Energy Plates could do anything beneficial for them. However, time and again, skeptics have been amazed once they took the chance and bought a Tesla Purple Energy Plate or disc for themselves. Authors such as Linda Goodman have certainly helped spread the word on just how fantastic the Tesla Purple Plates are.

Ralph Bergstresser - Inventor of the
Tesla Purple Plates.

Linda Goodman's Star Signs

In her highly acclaimed book, *"Star Signs,"* Linda Goodman spoke about energy fields and energy vibrations of the human body. Our liver may resonate at one frequency level, and the pancreas at another. This is the "life force energy responsible for universal harmony and synchronicity. This life force can get out of balance with stress, poor diet, or environmental toxins.

There are many ways to tune into this universal energy or life force. One of them is a Nikola Tesla-inspired discovery that Linda Goodman called the purple energy plates. The purple plates are anodized aluminum plates - they have been coated with a protective film by electrolytic means. They have been anodized with the color Violet, considered the healing ray of the rainbow spectrum. The atomic structure of the plates has been altered, so that they resonate to a high-frequency vibration. The purple energy plates possess a field of energy capable of penetrating any living thing - human, plant or animal with extraordinary results.

The healing effect of the purple plates Linda Goodman found most remarkable was the reduction of pain. If you place a purple plate on a bum, cut, or bruise, the healing is noticeably accelerated, and the pain is either greatly reduced or goes away completely Food items placed on the plate vibrationally increase in life force energy neutralizing the ill effect of lower vibrations i.e. pesticides, herbicides, grocery store scanning, chlorine.

This does not mean that those elements are not present; it simply means that a higher vibration has neutralized a lower vibration. It is like walking into a dark room. The pervading vibration is dense and low, which we identify as darkness. If we go over and switch on the lights…that is a higher vibration we call light. This lit room seemingly neutralizes or supersedes the vibration of darkness.

This is a basic example how a higher vibration neutralizes a lower vibration. The Positive Energy Products are a manifestation of Tesla's dream of "free energy" for us all. The seed was planted and grew to fruition through Ralph and has now been passed on to Earth Elements to benefit the user in a thousand ways.

Linda Goodman also writes of the plates ability to influence people in incredible ways. Within the more than dozen pages pertaining to Purple Plates in her book, Goodman writes that the plates possess the power to influence a person through the use of a photograph placed face down on the surface.

She uses the example of a friend's husband who was an alcoholic prone to negative behavior, and who was badly in need of a positive influence. Soon after using the husband's photograph on the purple plate, he began a recovery which included sobriety and hopefulness.

However, Goodman, as well as others, warn that leaving a photograph on the plate for any more than 15 minutes to a half hour at a time can cause nervousness or anxiety in some people. She also warns that attempting to influence a person in a negative fashion will not work.

Concern About Protection From Electromagnetic Pollution

Electromagnetic radiation is the complete range of wavelengths generated by the oscillation of electric charges. Everything from cell phones, mobile phones, cellular phones, and a pocket radio to power lines and everything in-between emits EMR. You cannot see it but you can feel it.

Put the back of your forearm next to a TV screen or a computer monitor and feel the hairs on your arm move. The field of the TV or computer monitor's EMR induced an electrical field in the biological tissue of the: hair on your arm.

But is EMR a health hazard? Worldwide reports on scientific studies regarding EMR continue to reach us. Government bodies, major industrial corporations and scientific researchers spend billions of dollars in search for conclusive evidence as to exactly what EMR does to the health of humanity.

While the investigations continue the public's fear of power lines and microwave towers near schools and homes continues to grow. The increasing number of cellular phone users joins computer operators in their concern over EMR cancer scares. Why the growing concern? From Japan we hear that it is generally accepted that microwave ovens are harmful to humans. Manufactures of microwave ovens take measures to protect the users from the health hazards of leaking microwaves. Mobile phones use microwaves.

From the United States we hear that researchers in Seattle discovered DNA damage in the brains of rats that had been exposed to radiation. Elsewhere rats were found to lose the ability to acquire simple tasks when exposed to a mere 45 minutes of microwave radiation.

In Australia the National Radiological Protection Board studied the effects of cell phone electromagnetic signals. Almost half of all the mice exposed to the signals developed cancer after just one and a half years.

In England thirty-three percent of scientists on one project stopped using their cell phones after their experiments with cellular phone signals. In July 1998 scientists at England's Defense Establishment Research Agency were working on a slice of a rat's brain. The slice was from the short-term-memory portion of the brain. The scientists stimulated the cells to make them function and then proceeded to broadcast radio signals.

The signals they used were at a lower level than is currently safe in cell phones. Within minutes their equipment showed readings that indicated the equivalent response of sudden memory loss and confusion in a living rat. The readings returned to normal once the signal was switched off.

The project director, Dr. Rick Hold said, "This is the first real evidence that these radio waves do have an effect on the brain. We cannot say whether, at this stage, this is dangerous or not - but clearly we need to find out pretty quickly."

The English scientists advised using caution when making the leap between experimental effects on rodents and what the same effects would be on humans. But as more research is conducted, the evidence seems to indicate that exposure to radio waves can be harmful.

In 1997, health science reporter Lila Lazarus wrote that Doctor Thomas Bauld, a biomedical engineer at U of M, made a similar statement. He said, "You have a whole issue in the differences in metabolism of the animal, differences in the blood circulation levels in different parts of their body or the fur or the other type of things that could impact whether or not you can transfer this. It's not an easy thing to do."

Nonetheless we continue to see disturbing reports. We read about new research suggesting that signals disrupt pans of the brain in charge of memory and learning. Cellular phones reportedly are causing a rise in blood pressure, may harm pregnant women, cause brain tumors, cancer, headaches and tiredness.

Scientist Dr. Roger Coghill has been quoted as saying, "Anyone who uses a cell phone for more than 20 minutes at a time needs to have their head examined." He went on to say that during June and July this year no less than five separate laboratories had produced evidence that cell phones were hazardous when used to excess.

It seems now that Tesla Purple Energy Plates could be the perfect solution to help protect ourselves from electromagnetic pollution.

According to the inventor, the atomic structure of these aluminum plates has been altered, allowing the atoms and electrons of the aluminum to resonate in tune with the basic energy of nature, the same energy that causes the particles of even- atom and molecule to be in constant vibration. The underlying theory is that it also allows them to function as transceivers, neutralizing electromagnetic wave forms and other microwaves that are injurious.

Tesla Purple Energy Plates and discs are catching on fast with people concerned about exposure to computer monitors and TV sets, and especially cellular phone users who are worried about the possible effects of radiation on brain tissues and other cells. Even particularly insensitive individuals have reported "hot spots" or headaches when cell phones are used for more than a couple of minutes, and news media reports indicate the scientific jury is still out about the degree of harm that could be involved. However, users of cellular phones report a marked reduction of these unpleasant effects when a Purple Energy Plate is attached to the back of the phone as close to the antenna as possible.

There are many uses for the Tesla purple plates. Here are only a few suggestions. With continued personal use you'll discover countless others.

- Place a small sized plate in a pocket or purse for more energy. (No body contact is necessary.

- Place large plate in refrigerator (center shelf is best.) Food, with the exception of fresh meat and fish, will stay fresh longer.

- Place beneath sick house plants, or water sick plants with water which has been placed on plate overnight.

- Place small plate in dog or cat bed, or under food dish.

- To energize crystals, place on purple plate for 12 hours.

- Use the plate on injured area of any living thing.

- Travelers can carry a small plate to energize their drinking water and eliminate illness and stomach upsets.

- Small plate placed on forehead to alleviate headache pain, on joints to alleviate gout and arthritis pain, on stomach to stop nausea.

- Placed on forehead to help remember dreams and to promote deeper meditation.

TESLA'S LOST SCIENCE – PURPLE ENERGY PLATES

Upon the passing of Nikola Tesla in 1943, dozens of trunks containing his private journals and unpatented inventions were retained by the Custodian of Alien Properties and were locked away. From inside information gathered in the years following his death, it was ascertained that officials from Wright-Patterson Air Force Base (also the home for many years of Project Blue Book, headquarters of the government's UFO cover-up attempt) hurried to the warehouses of the Custodian of Alien Properties and took possession of all of Tesla's documents and other materials, all of which were classified at the highest level.

To this day, a great deal of Tesla's papers remains in government hands and are still highly classified. There are literally tons of notes, documents, drawings, and plans, as well as over twenty boxes of reportedly "missing" Tesla material. The government distributed false rumors that Tesla never kept notes, which is a blatant lie. Over the course of time – largely in the last decade – some of Tesla's lost journals have been uncovered, and a number of his "secret inventions" have been privately developed. One of these inventions is Tesla's Purple Harmony Generator – also known as Tesla's Purple Energy Plate. Though the "generators" have been around for a number of years, they are only now starting to receive the international attention they deserve in the alternative energy field.

In an article published in the August 2000 edition of the popular FATE magazine, author Corrie DeWinter mentions that she first became aware of the generators while reading a book called "*Star Signs*" by Linda Goodman.

Goodman mentions that the person who created the plates with Tesla preferred to remain anonymous. However, after the inventor's death, the company which produced the plates decided to give him due credit. The inventor, Ralph Bergstresser was born in 1912 in Pueblo, Colorado, of German parents who immigrated to the United States.

He was extremely interested in free energy or Zero Point Energy as it is now called in scientific circles. Bergstresser carefully studied anything written about Nikola Tesla's experiments, and attended many lectures given by Tesla. At one point they were introduced and quickly became friends, due to their shared interest in free energy.

According to the FATE article, Bergstresser continued with his work for many years and following Tesla's death came into possession of several notebooks which helped him further develop the harmony plates. For all intents and purposes the plates look innocent enough.

Coming in a variety of sizes, they are purple in color and are said to be..."In resonance, or in tune, with the basic energy of the universe. They function as transceivers – creating a field of energy around themselves that will penetrate any material substance by osmosis. The energy is very beneficial to all life… plant, animal, or human. It might be considered as Positive Energy."

Somehow or other – according to current thinking regarding the plates – the original atoms of the anodized aluminum structures are restructured when put through a proprietary process whereby the vibrational frequency of the atoms and electrons is changed.

Non-approved FDA testing has reportedly shown that the healing process is accelerated for burns and bone fractures when the injured party becomes the focal point of the purple plates' force field by wearing one of the self contained generators. Aches and pains are said to go away, the quality of sleep may be improved, water and food becomes more tasty (to establish this simply put a purple plate on a shelf in your frig.

The quality of cheap wine is remarkably enhanced. Plates have been placed under sick houseplants, and near the food dish of small pets. Corrie De Winter in her FATE article offers several suggestions for the use of the plates:

"Place a small-size plate in a pocket or purse for energy… small plate (is often) placed on forehead to alleviate headache pain, on joints to alleviate gout and arthritis pain, on stomach to stop nausea… Placed on forehead in the morning will help you to remember your dreams… I have also read testimonials from plate users who claim they help with cramps, headaches, stomach upsets, stiff joints, torticollis, swelling, ringworm, 'clicking' jaw, alcoholism, anxiety, colic and depression."

Probably one of the most influential tests has been conducted by the Perrysburg School District allowing them to stop using dangerous pesticides around the Frank Elementary School pupils and very naturally by utilizing the Tesla generators or plates.

According to the school custodian, the plates where installed in the cafeteria and elsewhere around the building allowing them to greatly control the pest population. One of the most commonly used pesticides was developed by Hitler in World War II to penetrate mustard gas masks... the purple plates provide a totally safe means to attack the problem of pests.

Tesla may have been able to observe that under specific conditions the inter-relationships between time, space, gravity, electromagnetic and subatomic forces can become interpenetrable in terms of a unified energy system.

POSITIVE ENERGY PLATES

By Roy Kupsinel, M.D.

Originally published in *Health Consciousness*, October 1991

They function as transceivers...creating a field of energy around themselves that will penetrate any material substance. This energy is very beneficial (the life-force energy) to all life ... plant, animal or human.

Everything in the Universe is energy and vibration. Each basic element of the known atomic chart consists of energy at different rates of vibration. The difference between gold and silver is due to the difference in atomic structure and vibration rates.

There is a frequency or vibration of energy that saturates the Universe. This energy is beneficial to all living cells whether human, plant or animal. Man has the power to utilize this energy "with his mind." Every thought is transmitted by this energy...this basic energy of the Universe. This energy might be considered the basic power of the Universe...or God. God is everything, everywhere. The power behind the thought is "energy," or call it God Power or Creative Power...or Prana in Yoga philosophy. The Breath of Life, the Holy Spirit is this energy.

Spiritual growth is our only purpose and reason for being alive on earth. Each individual must learn how to utilize this energy for spiritual growth and constructive purposes. Constructive use (positive use) of this energy raises the level of consciousness of man...or raises his vibration rate or frequency. Every individual has a different rate of vibration. All of man's earthly problems are created by his thought projections. What we project from our mind in the form of thoughts, we create and receive. Spiritual growth requires "overcoming all negative thinking," which dissipates "the life force" or vital energy.

The energized plates are to help mankind raise his vibrational rate. The atomic structure of these aluminum plates has been altered with man-made equipment. The atoms and electrons of the aluminum have been altered so that the plates are in resonance, or in tune, with the basic energy of the Universe. They function as transceivers, creating a field of energy around themselves that will penetrate any material substance. This energy is very beneficial (the life-force energy) to all life...plant, animal or human. It might be considered as Positive Energy, or as God power. Love is "positive energy." God is love. God is energy.

Science has proven that by projecting "love," or positive energy, to a plant, the plant will flourish and grow vigorously. If a child is injured, its mother will project love (positive energy) to the child...by laying her hands on the painful area. She automatically releases "energy," or "prana" in Yoga, and the pain is relieved. The plates can do the same thing when placed upon an injured area of man, plant or animal.

If a person receives a burn, they have suddenly changed the normal vibrational rate of the tissue, and they suffer pain. The plates will help to quickly return the burned area back to its normal rate of vibration...and the pain will usually be relieved or disappear. All faith healing utilizes this energy.

These plates will help to raise the vibrational rate of any individual using them. In no way, can these plates be harmful. The plates seem to neutralize anything negative in food or water. Many people place their food on the large plates when they are still in paper sacks from the market. The time required is about fifteen minutes. Plate energy will change the taste of wine...and for some reason, cheap wine improves and expensive wine becomes like vinegar. A glass of water may become energized in two or three minutes by setting it on a plate. Travelers in foreign countries energize their drinking water and eliminate illness and stomach upset from water changes. A plate that is placed on top, or under, a vodka martini, will ruin the martini...it will taste like water. Time required...about two or three minutes. Coffee changes taste, cigarettes become milder, pineapple becomes sweet (and not sour tasting).

When the plates are placed upon burns, cuts, aches and pains in the human body, healing appears to be accelerated and the pain lessens or disappears entirely. This is accomplished by returning the injured cells or tissue back to their normal vibrational rate. Healing is accomplished by bringing the area back into proper balance.

These plates have been channeled to Earth from the higher realms (spiritual world) to benefit mankind and to help relieve his suffering at this time (the twilight hours before the Dawn of a New Age.) The violet color represents the 7th Ray (and the violet flame of St. Germain). The color (vibration) is very beneficial to obtain the desired results.

Some people sleep on these plates by placing them under their mattress ... and this helps to give them more energy and raise their vibrational rate. Other people cannot sleep with the plates near them, as they will remain awake most of the night. By wearing the small plate in a pocket, most people will feel an increase of energy and less fatigue.

Plates that have been in use for more than fifteen years ... are still functioning very well after that length of time. Once the structure of the atoms of the aluminum has been altered, they will remain in that condition ... possibly indefinitely. Plates are not "charged." They are utilizing the basic energy of the Universe, or free energy.

PLATE APPLICATIONS

- Wear the small plate in pocket for more energy. If no pockets, women carry the plates in their purse (no body contact necessary).

- Place purchased bags of food on the large plate (approx. 15 minutes). This induces the "life force energy" and helps neutralize anything negative.

- Place large plate in refrigerator (center shelf). Food will last much longer (except for fresh meat and fish), and thermostat may have to be readjusted if food freezes.

- Place plate under sick house plants.

- Place small plate in dog or cat bed, or under food dish.

- To energize crystals or decomposed granite (or quartz sand), place material on the plate for 12 hours. Scatter quartz sand or granite onto indoor or outdoor trees or plants to enhance growth.

- Place one gallon of water on large or small plates and use to water plants (12 hours or overnight).

- Use the plate on injured area of any living thing.

KUP'S KOMMENT: During my recent visit to see Ralph Bergstresser (the inventor) I was amazed at the activity (at his factory) with his lovely and able female helper, Elizabeth. Orders for these Purple Energy Plates are pouring in from all over the world with frequent overseas telephone calls being received during the sleeping hours by the answer device.

While I was there, one customer called from India to ask, "Where is my order I mailed you three weeks ago?" Next day, the letter was delivered and off the order went via air mail! Seems most customers are into what we call in medicine, "primary process," which means, "I want what I want, and I want it now!"

After meeting Ralph for the first time in the mid 1980's I presented an article in the August 1986 HC, "*Energy Innovation Products*" by Ralph. Subsequently, I have been using the plates and his other products. I have introduced many people to them and they are universally appreciative.

By word of mouth, more and more people are obtaining these plates that are colored a specific purple color - that color of St. Germain.

In 1987 the book *"Linda Goodman's Star Signs: The Secret Codes of the Universe"* was published and has greatly helped spread the word of these plates on an international basis. Linda devoted an entire chapter to them.

Linda is a polished writer. Here's my very brief summary of the highlights from her book on the plates. From her personal experiences she has found them to be beneficial in specific cases:

Pain except from twisted muscles or slipped discs.

Migraine headache.

Dislocated arm.

Relief of nausea.

Increased energy.

"Broadcasting" (my term) of healing with Polaroid photos.

Other people have reported: Knee pain and swelling relieved in fifteen minutes.

Post partum (after childbirth) ovarian problem.

Asthmatic child.

Sinus headaches, cough, gagging and postnasal drip.

Colic.

Depression.

Now I'd like to share with you a few of the many experiences I have had with these plates. I carry one at all times in my shirt pocket or back pants pocket if none on the shirt. Whenever I eat, I place it under my beverage and/or food. My friend Henry B. Rosenberg of Bayonne, New Jersey frequently entertains his business contact throughout the country. When one orders a martini Henry places the plate underneath it and within a few minutes the martini is unpalatable. What a way to stop drinking.

Just last week, my friend Dr. Kea Lipke told me about his pineapple experience and said it looks like there really is something to these plates. Having read the material I sent him, he was served pineapple with his breakfast. After the initial bitter taste he placed the dish upon the energy plate and when he returned ten minutes later he was amazed to find the smooth sweet flavor.

Recently I had given Ken the plate at the University of Science and Philosophy Third Annual Homecoming in Charlottesville, Virginia at the Omni Hotel during my talk. Wearing metal-framed glasses, Ken volunteered to help me with the Behavioral Kinesology (BK) demonstration, a form of muscle testing I learned from John Diamond, MD (Read *"Your Body Doesn't Lie"* by J.D. for more info).

Metal crossing the midline, (e.g. cover the nose between the eyes) of the body causes a phenomena called "switching." When a person is switched there is an imbalance between the two hemispheres of the brain. The results may cause, to varying degrees, problems with memory, concentration, balance, coordination, receptivity and energy levels.

Using BK, I had Ken place his right hand (palm inward) opposite his right ear and extend his left upper extremity to the side and parallel to the floor. When I pushed on the outstretched extremity, it did not go down. Now, I had him place his right hand opposite his left ear and he went weak. Next, I placed the purple plate in his left shirt pocket, retested and he was strong. When I tested him without the glasses his cerebral hemispheres were in balance. The plate balanced the negative effect of the metal across the midline of the glasses.

Yesterday, I went to pick up my photos at International Camera here in Casselbery. A couple of weeks ago I did a similar demonstration on the owner, Albert, but Jimmy was on vacation. Like Albert, Jimmy was wearing metal-framed glasses.

First, I tested him just like I described for Ken. Then I told him to go out and walk in front of my parked car and come back in. Well, I then tested him (without the glasses). I asked him to extend his left upper extremity and when I pushed on it, it went down almost like pressing on butter. Then I placed the purple plate in his shirt pocket, tested and now he's strong.

If the testing is done when a person is switched, you get the opposite answer. Now, to explain! There is a negative forward energy in from of a car for eighteen minutes after the motor has been stopped. By walking in front of the car this force will weaken your body energy of vital life force. When you park, walk around behind. Also, if you wish to counteract this negative force, use the plate. Now one more bit about BK. There are various acupuncture alarm points on the body that can be tested in a similar manner as just described, only a finger is placed on the point and the outstretched upper extremity is pressed upon.

The acupuncture alarm point for the thyroid is just below the belly button or umbilicus. I have my patient place a right-hand finger there and extend his left upper extremity. If there is an energy imbalance with the thyroid, the extremity will be weak. Now, by placing the plate in the patient's pocket or on his/her body there will be no weakness.

Well, I could go on, but I don't want to put you to sleep. However, if you are going to sleep and wish to enhance your ability to recall dreams, put a small plate or two under your pillow or a large plate under your mattress. It works for me and others. Vitamin B6 also helps with dream recall.

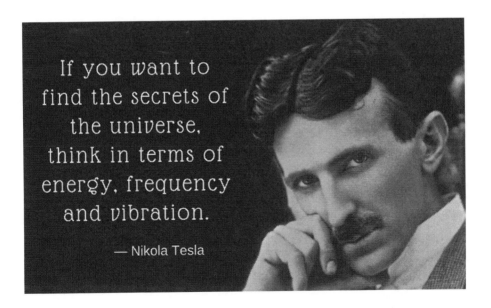

If you want to find the secrets of the universe, think in terms of energy, frequency and vibration.

— Nikola Tesla

PURPLE ENERGY PLATES – LEGACY OF NIKOLA TESLA

Nikola Tesla - the scientist who introduced the world to the alternating current technologies of electrical power generation, transmission, the radio technology we use and other innovations such as computer language, remote-control systems, and car engine starters, took considerable interest in crystalline materials. He collected the best scientific literature available at the time on crystalline materials – indeed, his holdings and articles located in the Tesla Museum in Belgrade on the subject are quite impressive.

As a result of such research, Nikola Tesla progressed onto advanced methods of refining materials from powdered ores. These novel extractive processes were successfully demonstrated to the best expert metallurgists of the day. His techniques did not require blast furnace operation and were demonstrable in room environment. Unfortunately, little is known about these demonstrations.

Nikola Tesla developed high-resolution X-ray devices that would permit himn to observe crystalline lattices in materials and to note how the configuration of these could be modified by the various energy emitting devices he designed – including his coils, his carbon button lamps and his exhausted or phosphorescent tube. We know that Tesla adamantly stood by certain concepts of atomic structure and inter-atomic activity, energy wave propagation, even to the point of publicly criticizing Albert Einstein, coming up with empirical data to back up his position. Evidently his statements were backed up by the certitude of observations made in numerous experiments.

Tesla actually developed an electron microscope that allowed him to observe effects on materials induced through his high-energy devices (so had greater energy density than our nuclear reactors), decades ahead of his time.

It was with this research direction, high-energy sources and advanced monitoring systems that Nikola Tesla was in a position to uncover the methodology to molecularly re-structured materials. Molecules can be re-organized either internally and between themselves and certain energy sources can modify these critical molecular relationships. For example, pharmaceuticals have "expiry" dates due to the changes in these molecular bonds. The re-structured materials based on Nikola Tesla's research and technologies provide new scientific and technological opportunities.

Tesla developed a process of de-gasifying, refining and purifying materials. One of his methods was sold to the American Smelting and Refining Company in the early 1930s. Dr. A. J. Phillips, superintendent of the company stated that $25,000 was invested in the novel process. A similar process, developed more extensively by Tesla, was investigated with due diligence by John G. Trump, a M. I. T. engineer commissioned by the United States National Defense Research Committee (NDRC).

After Tesla died in 1943, Trump (paternal uncle of President Donald Trump), on behalf of the Office of Scientific Research and Development spent less than two days examining the contents of 30 trunks that belonged to Tesla.

Trump's examination was accompanied by John Newington (New York City office of the Office of Alien Property), Charles Hedetniemi, OAP Washington representative, Willis George of the Office of Naval Intelligence and Edward Palmer, John Corbett, both with the United States Marine Reserves.

Another researcher, Bloyce Fitzgerald, who also worked at M.I.T., and a protégé of Nikola Tesla, gained access to Tesla's research on open-ended vacuum tubes. Such tubes – and other Tesla apparatus were able to attain voltages of up to 50,000,000 volts, used to yield very small particles in concentrated, non-dispersive rays. By the 1920s, these tubes were the core of Tesla's high-energy beam technology. As early as 1894, Tesla achieved dematerialization through radiant energy emissions. Tesla found, and reported to, engineering institutions that he could dematerialize highly polished carbon, diamonds and other crystalline materials, including rubies.

Also in 1894, Tesla achieved laser effects by forcing energy into the non-linear medium of not only solid rubies but also the even-still-more highly non-linear media of molten ruby drops. Clearly, he was aware of the technological implications of plasma in non-linear physics. So perhaps Tesla was able to observe that under specific conditions the inter-relationships between time, space, gravity, electromagnetic and subatomic forces can become interpenetrable in terms of a unified energy system.

Purple Plates – A High Energy Research Legacy

There exist curiosity items – Purple Plates – that are directly linked to Tesla's scientific achievements in the use of high-energy emissions. These are the legacy of experience obtained by individuals who enjoyed direct and privileged access to Nikola Tesla's laboratory work.

The items are made with materials characterized by naturally orderly lattices – such as aluminum, sand and certain plastics. These lattices are energetically forced into a still more homogenous and regular patterns and molecular characteristics. There is reason of believe that mono-polarity is obtained within these treated solids and that the special states achieved therein are transferable to surrounding media - gaseous, liquid or solid, organic or inorganic.

In the public domain since the 1970s, these items have been applied by tens of thousands of users worldwide. Reported observations include: neutralization of acidific properties of water and other liquids (such as wines), imparting of new properties of gases such as ionization. The freezing points of liquids are temporarily altered in the proximity to the treated lattices.

The Purple Plates are also known as "energy plates." They were commercially introduced by Ralph Bergstresser, an aide to Nikola Tesla, appointed by President Roosevelt along with Bloyce Fitzgerald, during the last months of his life in the 1940s. Declassified FBI documents produced around the time of Tesla's death note that Bergstresser had warned the FBI about his fears that foreign countries may be targeting Tesla to either kidnap him or steal his work. Because of these warnings, the FBI kept agents living in the New Yorker hotel to keep a close eye on Tesla.

After his retirement in the 1970s, Ralph Bergstresser drew upon his lab experience with Tesla to generate a wide range of innovative consumer products using this high-energy technology: refreshers for refrigerators, plant-life boosters, water softeners, water-coolers for air-conditioning, fossil fuel economizers, life energy helpers and even chlorine-free swimming-pool maintenance. Consumer feedback also reported widespread accelerated wound and sore healing, headache and pain relief in the presence of the molecularly restructured materials. These items have been particularly well received by environmentally sensitive materials. Also pet lovers had their say on "miracles."

The desire that guides me in all I do is the desire to harness the forces of nature to the service of mankind.

Nikola Tesla

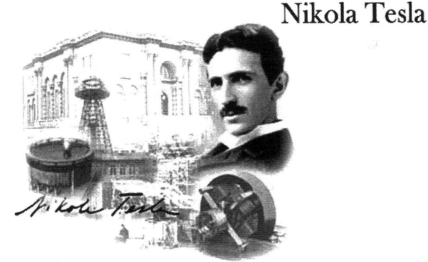

ELECTRO-THERAPY: THE FORERUNNER OF THE PURPLE ENERGY PLATES

Nikola Tesla (1856–1943) is one of the most fascinating and enigmatic electrical inventors of the late nineteenth and early twentieth century's. A brilliant though somewhat erratic man, at the height of his career he commanded the respect of engineers around the world, hobnobbed with New York's leading literati, and was hailed as a wizard by the general public and the media. Yet he ended his life in penury and isolation, feeding pigeons in his hotel room.

No history of the development of electrical technology could afford to ignore Tesla's seminal contributions to the generation, distribution, and utilization of ac power. Tesla's polyphase system is the basis for today's large-scale electric power networks, and his 40 patents in this area, conceived and developed between 1878 and 1888, represent more than one third of his total patent output. These patents, particularly the first seven, granted together on May 1, 1888, were absolutely fundamental to ac power development. Two weeks after the patents were issued; Tesla was invited to speak to the American Institute of Electrical Engineers, where on May 16 he gave his first public lecture on his startling discoveries.

43

George Westinghouse immediately realized their importance and purchased the first seven and all of Tesla's subsequent polyphase patents, which covered both synchronous and induction motors, and he used them to develop a practical electrical power system at Niagara Falls in the 1890's. Thus, Tesla helped launch the modern era of electric light and power while still in his thirties, his most creative and productive period. He was later and appropriately honored when the unit of magnetic induction, or magnetic flux density, was named the "Tesla."

Tesla's pioneering work on ac electrical systems is well known and is reasonably well documented by historians of technology, given the limitations of the available primary sources. Interested readers should consult Hughes' magisterial Networks of Power: Electrification in Western Society, 1880–1930 and Kline's article on the induction motor in Technology and Culture. Less well understood is his later, often quite spectacular work on high-frequency currents that he launched in the early 1890's.

Electrotherapy has a fascinating, if somewhat checkered history. The modern era of electrotherapy dates from the eighteenth century, when efficient electrostatic generators and storage devices were invented. Benjamin Franklin, for instance, used static electricity to treat paralysis, though with ambiguous results. However, other less careful or less scrupulous researchers were all too willing to make broad claims for their electrical "cures," and the field acquired the odor of quackery. The invention of the battery, the induction coil, and the magneto in the early nineteenth century added important new tools to electrotherapy, but it remained a somewhat suspect branch of medicine.

In the latter part of the nineteenth century, researchers such as Beard and Rockwell tried to bring order and scientific method to electrotherapeutics (with only partial success). Beard and Rockwell published their classic text, A Practical Treatise on the Medical and Surgical Uses of Electricity, in 1871, and it was reprinted numerous times. In fact, Rockwell was one of the participants in the September 1898 meeting of the American Electro-Therapeutics Association at which Tesla's paper was read.

As its president, Dr. C. R. Dickson, noted in the report on the meeting, the Association had been founded eight years earlier by those who "felt, and felt strongly, that electricity had been left too long to the charlatan, the incompetent and the unscrupulous."

The renewed interest in electrotherapy was also stimulated by the revolutionary discoveries in science and technology that characterized the last years of the nineteenth century. Crookes' cathode-ray tube, Hertz's demonstration of electromagnetic waves, Roentgen's discovery of X rays, and Thomson's discovery of the electron, to name a few, opened up new lines of research and provided new tools that could be added to the physician's "armamentarium electricum," as Dr. Dickson called it.

To contemporaries, society in general seemed to have been being transformed by electricity. Nowhere was this more apparent than in Buffalo, NY, where the Electro-Therapeutics Conference was held. Known as the "Electrical City," Buffalo derived its power from the ac dynamos at Niagara Falls, made possible in large part by Tesla's inventions. Tesla's prolific high-frequency inventions added another set of potential weapons to the armamentarium electricum. Tesla was one of the first electrical engineers to pay special attention to the physiological effects of high-frequency, high-tension currents.

Discovering that he could induce rapid heating in metal bars, even melting them, Tesla observed that living tissues also could be heated. He further noted the peculiar fact that humans can endure high-frequency currents of extremely high voltage without apparent harm. These characteristics suggested to Tesla and others that such currents might be of medical use. Thus was launched a new therapeutic modality that later became known as diathermy.

In the paper that follows, Telsa outlines a rich array of methods for producing different kinds of high frequency currents in order to produce various physiological effects—high voltage/low current, low voltage/high current, currents transmitted through space, etc. This is evidence of Tesla's technical brilliance and his ability to manipulate and push the available technology to its limits.

Safety was a major concern of Tesla's, and he addresses it at some length in this paper, perhaps worried that enthusiastic physicians with little knowledge of electricity might do more harm than good to their patients. He noted, for instance, that he once subjected himself to overly strong currents that induced warmth and perspiration in only a few seconds, followed by "an immense fatigue" that was greater than any he had ever experienced (though he felt fine the next day). He apparently did quite a bit of self experimentation, but he notes that he was never so fearful as when he placed his head within a coil that he had earlier used to fuse a sheet of tin.

Although Tesla generally deferred to physicians regarding the therapeutic aspects of electricity, in typical fashion he could not resist issuing bold speculations about possible medical uses.

In an earlier article, he proposed that the warming effects of high-frequency, high-voltage currents might be used to treat certain diseases. This was reasonable and modest enough, but he then went on to note that "it is conceivable that a person entirely nude at the North Pole might keep himself comfortably warm in this manner."

In his 1898 paper, he made the reasonable suggestion that the heating of metal pieces embedded in a body subjected to high voltages might yield new surgical techniques for sterilizing wounds or for locating and extracting metal objects. Yet he also suggested in this paper that millions of volts of electricity applied to a body would instantly throw off small particles of dust and dirt and constitute a new method of personal hygiene. This method "would be an efficient and time-saving substitute for a water bath" and might also be used for treating groups of patients at the same time, as in a hospital.

Tesla worried that due to his interest in using electricity and electromagnetism to treat physical illnesses, some might take him for a quack. Tesla once wrote: "a serious worker cannot despise anything more than the misuse and abuse of electricity which we have frequent occasion to witness." However, there is evidence that he was often approached by people wanted to be healed by

his miraculous discoveries. Thus it is not surprising that when money became tight (and it often was for Tesla), his associates urged him to produce electrotherapeutic devices for sale, such as a medical coil and something called the "Tesla Pad."

Though he may have resisted such commercialization, Tesla was undoubtedly sincere in his belief in the physical and mental benefits of what he called the "cold fire." He apparently used regular electric treatments on himself to alleviate depression.

As he once said, "You see, electricity puts into the tired body just what it most needs—life force, nerve force. They promote heart action and digestion, induce healthful sleep, rid the skin of destructive exudations and cure colds and fever by the warmth they create. They vivify atrophied or paralyzed parts of the body, allay all kinds of suffering and save annually thousands of lives. It's a great doctor, I can tell you, perhaps the greatest of all doctors."

Nikola Tesla also contributed to the science of ultrasound. In an attempt to remove the sound vibrations that hindered the use of alternating current for the arc lamp, he constructed a high-frequency alternator, which, in turn, led him to the study of the properties of ultrasound. In the winter of 1891 Tesla revealed that rapid oscillation currents can cross the human body without causing any muscle spasms or tissue damage.

Tesla claimed to have come to this conclusion by experimenting on his own body. The scientific world was soon informed of the fascinating properties of Tesla's currents. In New York, London and Paris Tesla performed a famous experiment with a lighted pipe in his hand, having been exposed himself to currents of 50,000 volts. The experiment was echoed as a sensation and hinted at the possibility of therapeutic application of high frequency current and voltage. High-frequency currents are obtained using the so called Tesla Coils, and his experimental evidence that they may pass through the human body without any danger opened a wide range of their applications in electrotherapy, magnetotherapy and thermotherapy as well as the possibilities for exploitation until now unexplored and insufficiently explained Tesla's radiant energy of high voltage electrostatic fields.

Tesla was primarily interested in these currents (20–40 kHz) so as to solve the problem of lighting and remote transmission of electricity, but he noted that, using the aforementioned, without any danger can be warmed up tissues inside the human body.

High Frequency Oscillators for Electro-Therapeutics

In 1898, Tesla published a paper that he read at the eighth annual meeting of the American Electro-Therapeutic Association in Buffalo, NY entitled, "High Frequency Oscillators for Electro-Therapeutic and Other Purposes." He states that "One of the early observed and remarkable features of the high frequency currents, and one which was chiefly of interest to the physician, was their apparent harmlessness which made it possible to pass relatively great amounts of electrical energy through the body of a person without causing pain or serious discomfort."

Coils up to three feet in diameter were used for magnetically treating the body without contact, though ten to a hundred thousand volts were present "between the first and last turn."

Preferably, Tesla describes using spheres of brass covered with two inches of insulating wax for contacting the patient, while unpleasant shocks were prevented.

Tesla concludes correctly that bodily "tissues are condensers" in the 1898 paper, which is the basic component (dielectric) for an equivalent circuit only recently developed for the human body.

In fact, the relative permittivity for tissue at any frequency from ELF (10 Hz-100 Hz) through RF (10 kHz-100 MHz) exceeds most commercially available dielectrics on the market.

This unique property of the human body indicates an inherent adaptation and perhaps innate compatibility toward the presence of high voltage electric fields, probably due to the high transmembrane potential already present in cellular tissue. Tesla also indicates that the after-effect from his coil treatment "was certainly beneficial" but that an hour exposure was too strong to be used frequently. This has been found to be still true today with the Tesla coil therapy devices.

On September 6, 1932, at a seminar presented by the American Congress of Physical Therapy, held in New York, Dr. Gustave Kolischer announced: "Tesla's high-frequency electrical currents are bringing about highly beneficial results in dealing with cancer, surpassing anything that could be accomplished with ordinary surgery."

Tesla was very proud of his contributions to electrotherapy, noting that "leaders in the profession have assured me that I have done more for humanity by this medical treatment than all my other discoveries and inventions."

Tesla's 1898 paper highlights the fact that some of the leading electrical researchers of a century ago were intensely interested in understanding the role of electricity in the body and how artificially produced currents affect human health. These questions remain relevant today.

**Original Caption: "Nikola Tesla holding in his hands balls of flame."
Tesla's accident in 1895 may have led to his later Dynamic Theory of
Gravity in which gravity is described as a "field effect." The presence
of highly charged, rotating magnetic fields could therefore influence
time/space within a localized area.**

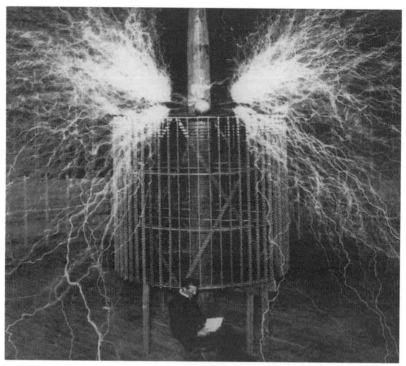

ABOVE: Tesla, in Colorado Spring's laboratory (1899), seated in front of the operating transformer.

BELOW: Tesla instrument to receive radio waves (1896).

The AMA's Battle with Electricity

Most scholars admit that Nikola Tesla made valuable contributions to the medical field with his pioneering work with X-rays. Today, we use X-rays in a great deal of medical procedures that require the need to further analyze the condition of patients in areas that are not immediately visible to the human eye. This breakthrough in medicine was made possible by the development of radio, wireless transitions of energy, the discovery of rays that could help penetrate the human tissue, and the use of Tesla currents in medical procedures. With these various types of practices and inventions, Nikola Tesla was able to effectively make his mark on the medical industry, most of which still exists in the equipment and practices we use today.

Even though many doctors and hospitals in the early 20th century used Tesla's methods for electro-therapy, the devices eventually fell out of favor when educators in western medical schools chose to only teach medical students in the use of pharmaceuticals and surgery. In addition, a concerted effort by the pharmaceutical industry and the AMA to discredit electromagnetic therapy caused it to be branded as "quackery" and electrical medical devices were only to be considered for diagnostic purposes such as X-ray. Tesla's advances were quickly forgotten.

All of this stems from 1910, when the Carnegie Foundation created The Flexner Report for the American Medical Association(AMA) that provided a detailed overview of preferred medical education in North America. Eventually the AMA designated a list of authorized medical schools and forbid the teaching of electrotherapy. Anyone using Tesla's magnetic coils for a medical therapy where considered to be "quacks."

Unfortunately, to this very day, doctors are still taught that electromagnetic fields have no "health" effect on the human body.

In North America, the practice of magnetic field therapy went deep underground; the schools that taught it were closed and electricians found jobs in traditional industries but the "war of medicine" continued. Many world-renowned doctors felt the AMA had wronged their practice of medicine. In 1932, at a seminar presented by the American Congress of Physical Therapy, Dr. Gustave Kolischer announced: "Tesla's high-frequency electrical currents are bringing about highly beneficial results in dealing with cancer, surpassing anything that could be accomplished with ordinary surgery."

In 1963, congressional hearings on "quack" devices forced companies that manufactured legitimate electrotherapy products into bankruptcy and the FDA put tight restrictions on electromagnetic medical devices. Medical "quack" doctors were barred from the AMA. Person's that practiced frequency therapy were put in jail for practicing medicine without a license. The pharmaceutical industry was now the dominating force with Valium, discovered in 1960, becoming the most prescribed drug in history. The public has now seen where all this has let to: the drug companies make over 1.2 trillion dollars per year.

After Tesla's death in 1943, his remaining research papers were sent to family members in Serbia and this was eventually confiscated by the Nazi's briefly during the WWII. During the following years of the cold war with the West, the Soviet Union embraced Tesla's methods of electromagnetic field therapy, preferring it to pharmaceuticals and surgery.

Soviet scientists then refined Tesla's medicine of frequencies, waveform shapes and methods of application to support their medical system. Electromagnetic fields were now "pulsed" making them much more effective. Tesla's name became a unit of measurement for the strength of the applied electromagnetic field. Extensive human trials in electrotherapy were done on entire select populations within the Soviet Union. Most hospitals and clinics offered some form of Tesla's electromagnetic field therapy because it worked so well with no side effects.

When the Berlin wall came down in 1990, the East Germans transferred Tesla's advanced soviet frequency therapy technology to West Germany. Government and private enterprises quickly realized that commercial interests from the west would suppress the miracles of Tesla's medicine. Neutral German-speaking countries such as Switzerland and Liechtenstein were chosen to provide production, distribution and corporate head offices. Brand new ultra-modern commercial and "home" versions of the large Russian hospital machines were sold as "wellness" devices.

With the invention of the Internet, the German-speaking companies then created websites in English to offer the sale of their devices directly to a worldwide public that had lost faith in their doctors and their prescribed pain medications that were no longer working.

In 2011, Dr. OZ, the popular television MD, discovered these Swiss made PEMF Bio-beds and he decided to go out on a limb and reintroduce Tesla's (PEMF) Pulsed Electromagnetic Field Therapy to his American TV audience. He stated in his opening remarks "I am more excited about this show than any other show I have done this season. Today, you are going to change the practice of medicine."

The healthcare agencies reacted to this new information too – and in a positive way. We now are quickly seeing these devices becoming legally licensed medical devices here in Canada and in the US they are offered as "wellness" devices. The last hurdle is to get "Tesla Medicine" accepted into the course curriculum of western medical universities so the doctors can prescribe it to their patents. That is the main purpose of the Healing Field documentary – to get Tesla therapy adopted into traditional forms of healthcare as a complimentary medicine. Magnetic fields make drugs more effective, you heal faster, pain free with fewer side effects.

These new developments with the ideas first conceived by Nikola Tesla more than one hundred years ago are exciting. People now have a chance to see for themselves how electrical therapy can be a superior treatment over drugs and surgery. Hopefully, the medical field in the United States will further embrace these techniques and we will see rapid development along with new ideas with health. All thanks to the pioneering work of Nikola Tesla.

THE THEORY BEHIND THE MULTIPLE WAVE OSCILLATOR

By Ralph Bergstresser

*NOTE: Ralph Bergstresser is the inventor of the Tesla Purple Energy Plates, based on experiments conducted by Nikola Tesla.

This article offers the theory of magnetic wave therapy using a Multiple Wave Oscillator (MWO). The Multiple Wave Oscillator is a tuned resonant system which is a multi-frequency generator. The basic idea for the original MWO came from the Russian scientist and bio-energetic pioneer, George Lakhovsky. He was inspired by the theories of Nikola Tesla, the inventor of high frequency/voltage technique. George Lakhovsky has elaborated these ideas with the help of Tesla. According to Lakhovsky the genes and chromosomes in all living cells are constantly in motion and function as small transmitters and receivers. Also, they have a resonant frequency that is due to size, shape and capacity.

MWO is based on bio-resonance whereby natural frequencies of cells, tissues, organs and the body are harmonized. MWO stimulates the self-healing ability of the body. When cells are exposed to a wide range of electromagnetic waves, they absorb the energy that matches their own resonance frequency.

In case of damage, complaints or illness there is always a disturbance or disruption in the vibration of the cells. MWO works quickly and directly on disturbed or disordered vibrations. Cells, tissues and organs are harmonized under the influence of electromagnetic fields and active in their own right frequency. This eliminates distortions and restores the natural balance in the body.

* * *

The use of high frequency/voltage at low current (in Amps) in living organisms such as plants, animals and people, has been the subject of medical interest for more than 60 years. Experiments with very high voltages have shown that physical pains can be treated very quickly and effectively, and often disappears within a few minutes. It is also found that infection and wounds heal very quickly.

These high frequencies and voltages cannot be applied directly to the body. The energy is passed through a gas-filled bulb (argon or neon). The molecules of the gas are brought into a very high vibration, and this high frequency goes to the point in the body where physical contact is made, without any kind of discomfort. There is no other manner in which this high energy might be tolerated by the cellular tissue.

Magnetic Wave Therapy has continuously developed over the last 30 years through repetitive experiments, improvements and optimizing the device. Especially the reactions, opinions and experiences of people using the equipment the current device have been established.

For example, a doctor in India had contact with a doctor in Jamaica and advised him not to take more than five minutes to allow the treatment in people with heart disease. The doctor gave it back to us. The reason was that cardiac patients often have a large amount of toxins in their bodies. The MWO, makes nitrogen very quickly be released from the cells of the body. If energy is supplied for too long, it is possible that the lymphatic system becomes overloaded. Drinking plenty of water (ionized) is therefore important, in order to discharge the formed waste through the kidneys. Beginning any treatment whatsoever for five minutes and see what the reaction is. Treat every day (antenna) and extend the time, each time by two minutes, until a total period of fifteen to twenty minutes has been reached. In a number of cases, a patient has a reaction like a rash or feeling tired. This means that the toxins are released from the body.

Hundreds of these devices are in use all over the world, and thousands of people have used it successfully. In America, there has done no scientific research so far. According to the information sources, this is due to the current medical system and the monopoly position which has its influence on all medical developments.

The friend that I have received the draft from has been through every conceivable opposition in America. They attempted to arrest him several times because of the device that was developed in its present form by him, because, according to the states, it could harm social and industrial interests.

The original device, the basic idea for the MWO therapy came from the Russian scientist, George Lakhovsky who worked around 1920 in Paris. The device of Lakhovsky was used in the twenties and thirties with great success in Europe.

This equipment was big, heavy and expensive, and thus only useful in hospitals. The present devices are easy to use, light in weight and compact. The equipment is reliable, durable and of better quality. This is much better than the old, original equipment, partly because there are very good methods to measure high voltages and frequencies.

The high frequency/voltage technique was invented around 1890 by Dr. Nikola Tesla, a truly brilliant scientist who has discovered alternating current (electricity at home, street lighting, etc.). A lot of equipment that makes use of this technique has since been placed on the market.

After 1925, the pharmaceutical and medical cartel using the most high-frequency/voltage equipment managed to eradicate. They found the drug approach much more lucrative. If someone is cured by an electrical appliance in a relatively short period, his medications are not profitable anymore. Many people I have talked with confirm this. The developer of this unit mentioned me, I know doctors who use the devices built by me. In the beginning they were very pleased with the quick and good results obtained by the MWO therapy. After some time, many stopped the treatment and were put back on medication because it was less time consuming and easier.

Fortunately, there are exceptions. A number of doctors have admitted that the MWO therapy is effective and that in many cases the patient has been cured after one or two treatments. When this happens, they lose a patient and thus revenue. In todays hectic time the therapists and doctors who work with this therapy, however, want a relief. The practice is often overloaded and you will see results that are often not thought to be possible.

Georges Lakhovsky in the Multiple Wave Oscillator field.

Below: Tesla had a hunch that high-potential, high-frequency currents could be passed into the body harmlessly, "these currents might lend themselves to elec-trotherapeutic uses." Tesla's suggestions were refined by George Lakhovsky who created his multiple-wave oscillator.

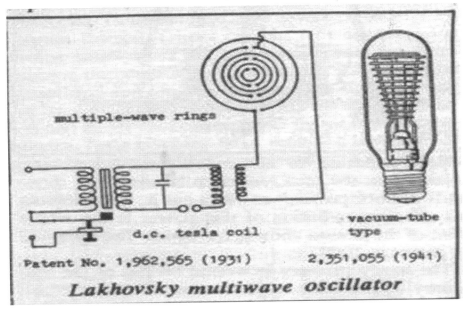

multiple-wave rings

d.c. tesla coil

vacuum-tube type

Patent No. 1,962,565 (1931)   2,351,055 (1941)

Lakhovsky multiwave oscillator

NIGHTMARES GONE, ALIEN INVASION DISPERSED, PLATES DISAPPEARING

Many strange things have happened to those owning the plates. One woman stated that she was having a series of nightmares when she started sleeping with one of the plates under her pillow. The dreams went from frightening to seeing her deceased father who she feels came to visit her from the spirit world. He was happy and joyful.

Others have reported having beneficial UFO encounters just by laying one of the large plates out in a field behind their home. This individual had been plagued by alien "bedroom invaders" who were coming into her house and wanting to have unwelcomed sexual intercourse. The "ETs"— or whoever they were – revised their plans after the confrontation with the purple plates nearby.

Another individual said they have heard reports of the purple plates & discs disappearing.

"I have studied theology and from a theological point of these plates really interest me. I have in my research come to find that according to ancient Mesopotamian teachings there are nine worlds each interrelated yet separate. Each more perfect than the next. Also Ancient Egyptian teachings confirm that there are nine dimensions.

"With this in view I believe we can find the explanation for the disappearance of the plates. It is highly possible that these plates resonate with the energy of a higher 'world' or dimension. A dimension in which pain and hurt and negativity do not exist.

Therefore if the plates are indeed a transceiver they merely convey this higher reality into our lesser own. So if they are indeed connected to a higher world or dimension it is highly likely then that they just disappear back into their higher world spontaneously. I'm also led to believe as you have subtly suggested on your site that these plates resonate energy of Absolute Love. The plates being purple (the color of royalty or spirituality to the Ancients) seem to be connected to the highest or ninth world. That world is the fullness of Love. This would account for the plates healing properties.

Signed, "Clinton."

TESTIMONIALS

So many people over the years have discovered the amazing Tesla Purple Energy Plates and have written in to voice their pleasure of this fantastic invention. Here are just a few testimonials that we would like to share.

• • •

"I first used a Purple Plate over twenty years ago. My Dad bought one for me and I've always been fascinated with them and kept one with me wherever I go. I started studying Reiki several years ago and am now a Reiki Master. I use healing energy all the time but had forgotten about the energy in the Purple Plates. I just got one yesterday from Purpleplates.Com and held it in my palm. I was amazed at the energy I could feel, even in a small pendant. I am impressed with the power of these Plates and am planning to make mine into a necklace to wear. I'm so glad that these wonderful Plates are still being made. You can carry the energy with you easily and always. I recommend these for purifying food and water as well. Thanks."

Shari Rood

We tested your small and large Purple Tesla Plates and found them superior to the competition. The large plate worked particularly well in keeping food fresh when placed at the bottom of the refrigerator."

-Verve Technology LLC, Sarasota, Florida, Charles Singer, CEO
"I want to tell you how much your products helped. I have a torn rotator cuff and it is painful and limits my motion. Within 24 hrs of wearing the quartz bracelet with purple disk the pain was completely gone. A boy who had brain surgery for a tumor and is now prone to headaches asked if he could use the small plate. It helped him and I gave it to him. Thank you for your time and help. Thank you for a miracle product."

Karen D. - NJ, USA

"I just received a purple plate pendant from a good friend of mine and I was a pretty huge skeptic and was sure this stuff was absolute crap, but I was wrong! Your product has really changed my life! Not only has it shown a profound effect on me, but I've noticed my family is now in a better mood and the vibes given off from this thing are showing that it is working, I also placed the plate under a cup of water and it made the water taste so much fresher and crisp. My 3-year-old cousin said something to me the other day that completely shocked me, she said she could feel the pendant shaking and it really freaked her out. Is there something that children can see and hear that us adults can't? I'm amazed! Thank you for this amazing product!"

Franklin T. MacDonald, Ashville, TN

"I have a story to tell you. I had been having my pain in my abdomen and was successfully using a Small plate to ease the pain before my scheduled surgery. I had to get X-rays of my torso area before the operation, and on the X-ray there was an illuminated rectangle area on the X-rays in the shape of the plate I had been using for the pain! The technician was mystified, but I knew exactly what it was – the energy was still there, helping with the pain. I found this to be amazing & now I have proof that the energy works! THANK YOU!"

Thomas Mc Nair, Washington, DC

I wanted to let you know that ever since I put the disks on my cats' collars, they seem to be getting along better! Alley is a feral TNR cat I bought in to live with us four years ago. I am totally convinced that the positive energy emanating from these disks is working! Alley and Ouija are friendlier with each other than I ever thought they would be! You've made a believer out of me, that's for sure.

Best, Judy

Hey Y'all,

Due to a situation that is outside of my control, I've been extremely tense and stressed for the last few months, and horribly irritable and argumentative with everybody. My stomach always hurts, my chest feels tight and I've had trouble breathing. I put the small plate on my belly and within a few minutes the pain was gone. Then I put the disk on my forehead covering my 3rd eye. I just kept feeling like I needed it there.

I was trying to figure out a way to keep it there with maybe a leather or elastic band and amazingly... it stayed there all by itself. I can turn my head, get up and walk around, shake and nod and it sticks. All day long I felt wrung out and all I wanted to do was cry. Every time I took it off I felt like I had to put it back. When I lay down to go to sleep I took it off figuring I'd for sure lose it in my sleep but I felt I had to put it back on. When I woke up this morning it was still there, stuck to my forehead and for the first time in months I FEEL GREAT! For the first time in months I'm not angry. The irritants are still there, just as annoying as ever, but they aren't bothering me today. I guess the disk will fall off when I don't need it anymore - I just have to remember to take it off before I go where anyone can see me. It does look a bit odd up there!

Thank you so much!
Theresa

Hello,

After using the plates for the first time yesterday, I woke up at such a high level of vibration I called three of my good friends and told them all about it. It's going to be fun to experience a continued flow on the airplane. Love this energy. We've got to find a way to light up our homes and offices with it as Tesla intended. I'm having fun putting photos of family and friends on the large plate for 15 minutes at a time, including some tribes I met in Africa during my photo safari there, and Indonesia. I know we can be the change we want to see, and live in a space where it's a win-win. We will get there and your products are supporting us.

Peace and blessings - stay forever young.

Ella Croney (Author of "*Stay Young Forever*")

I bought a small plate 2 months ago & put it in my wallet (having bad money problems) in hopes that it would help me gain money. Almost immediately I was getting funds that came from various sources, all unexpected. Since then I have not had money problems, thankfully! Also, my wallet was stolen (it had the plate in it still) and the next day they found the thief, and the wallet was returned with all the money that had been in it. I don't know if it was because of the plate, but I wouldn't be surprised!
Thank you SO much!!

Allison Murchie
Southampton, MA

A friend of mine recently got me a purple plate bracelet. I read about these in Linda Goodman's *"Star Signs."* Being a fan of Nikola Tesla also, it didn't take much for me to believe these plates work. Upon wearing my bracelet, I no longer have pain or discomfort in my wrist and i believe an old elbow injury is finally healing also. A friend of mine placed the bracelet against various parts of her body that NORMALLY are in pain and she was surprised to have instant relief. Your products are truly amazing and I have no doubt about their authenticity. Free energy really is the way of the future. Thanks so much for your work and dedication.

Sincerely, A.Tieff

I have owned a large and a small plate since 1994. I have found relief from minor aches, indigestion; also have felt re-energized after a tiring day. I have carried with me the smaller plate as I started a work day and felt more energy than usual throughout the day. I have used my plates to send positive energy to a person in distress by placing a picture or the negative on the plate, and definitely as suggested in Linda Goodman's book if the person is aware of what you are doing it has a more prompt, and effective. I have found that it can stimulate me too much if I try to sleep with it under my pillow, but I can put it under the mattress and was able to sleep well. I feel the plates have been very beneficial to me and would recommend them to anyone.

Sincerely and gratefully, M. Arantes.
Miami, Florida

During experiments at Colorado Springs in 1899, Tesla began to receive radio signals of an unusual nature. He would later write: "*Although I could not at the time decipher their meaning, it was impossible for me to think of them as having been entirely accidental. The feeling is constantly growing on me that I had been the first to hear the greeting of one planet to another. A purpose was behind these electrical signals.*"

"All people everywhere should have access to free energy sources. Electric power is everywhere, present in unlimited quantities and can drive the world's machinery without the need for coal, oil or gas."
- *Nikola Tesla*

New York 7, New York

65-12290
HR:mhm

CONFIDENTIAL
October 17, 1945

Director, FBI

Re: UNKNOWN SUBJECTS;
SAVA KOSANOVICH;
Experiments and research of NIKOLA TESLA (deceased)
ESPIONAGE — M

Dear Sir:

Reference is made to the Bureau letter dated January 21, 1943, which bore a caption similar to that mentioned above.

The referenced letter dealt with the death, on January 7, 1943, of the famous inventor, NIKOLA TESLA, who as well as being the inventor of Alternating Current, perfected many electrical devices. He is also credited with having developed the so called "death ray" which would safeguard any country from attack by air.

On June 9, 1945, a RALPH BERGSTRESSER of New York City furnished information of a nonspecific nature indicating that it was his belief that persons sympathetic to Russia were making an effort to secure the effects of NIKOLA TESLA in order to salvage therefrom any models or designs of possible military value. Mr. BERGSTRESSER claimed that he heard that ABRAHAM N. SPANEL, President of the NATIONAL LATEX CORPORATION, of Dover, Delaware was the motivating influence behind this attempt to obtain TESLA'S papers which are presently held in storage at the MANHATTAN STORAGE WAREHOUSE in New York City. BERGSTRESSER promised to return to the New York Field Division shortly after his initial visit and furnish further and more specific information to support his claims.

He was not heard from again, however, until September 27, 1945, at which time he furnished the following additional information:

He said that a boyhood chum of his from Wichita, Kansas, BLOYCE FITZGERALD, had been TESLA'S protege and one of the inventors few confidents. According to BERGSTRESSER, FITZGERALD who is now an Army Private stationed at Wright Field, Dayton, Ohio, is a brilliant 29 year old scientist who spent endless hours with TESLA prior to the latters death, during which time TESLA explained to him most secret experiments. BERGSTRESSER stated that FITZGERALD met TESLA in November 1942, but he had been corresponding with the latter since 1935. According to the informant, FITZGERALD had developed some sort of anti-tank gun, the details of which he presented to TESLA who made certain corrections in design and specifications to further perfect the weapon.

BERGSTRESSER related that sometime in December 1942, when FITZGERALD was attending a meeting of the AMERICAN SOCIETY OF MECHANICAL ENGINEERS, he made the acquaintance of ABRAHAM SPANEL who became interested in FITZGERALD'S

65-12290-18cor

Declassified FBI document from October 17, 1945 detailing Ralph Bergstresser's concern that Russia was trying to secure anything of possible military value from Tesla's notes and journals.

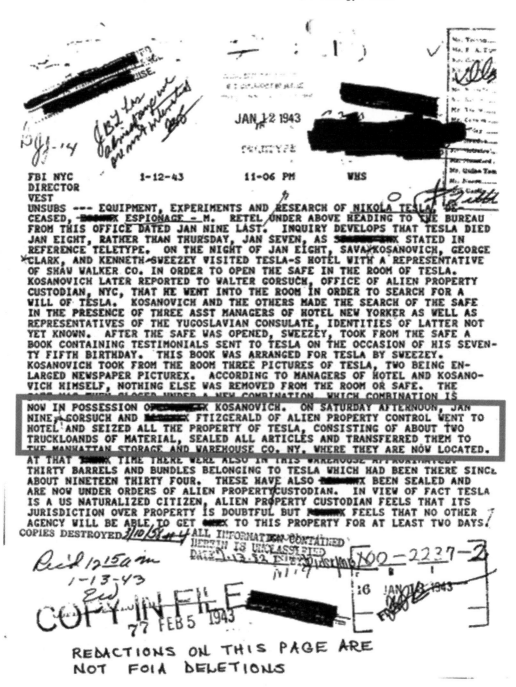

JAN 12 1943

FBI NYC   1-12-43   11-06 PM   WHS
DIRECTOR
VEST
UNSUBS --- EQUIPMENT, EXPERIMENTS AND RESEARCH OF NIKOLA TESLA, DE-
CEASED, ESPIONAGE - M. RETEL UNDER ABOVE HEADING TO THE BUREAU
FROM THIS OFFICE DATED JAN NINE LAST. INQUIRY DEVELOPS THAT TESLA DIED
JAN EIGHT, RATHER THAN THURSDAY, JAN SEVEN, AS STATED IN
REFERENCE TELETYPE. ON THE NIGHT OF JAN EIGHT, SAVA KOSANOVICH, GEORGE
CLARK, AND KENNETH SWEEZEY VISITED TESLA-S HOTEL WITH A REPRESENTATIVE
OF SHAW WALKER CO. IN ORDER TO OPEN THE SAFE IN THE ROOM OF TESLA.
KOSANOVICH LATER REPORTED TO WALTER GORSUCH, OFFICE OF ALIEN PROPERTY
CUSTODIAN, NYC, THAT HE WENT INTO THE ROOM IN ORDER TO SEARCH FOR A
WILL OF TESLA. KOSANOVICH AND THE OTHERS MADE THE SEARCH OF THE SAFE
IN THE PRESENCE OF THREE ASST MANAGERS OF HOTEL NEW YORKER AS WELL AS
REPRESENTATIVES OF THE YUGOSLAVIAN CONSULATE, IDENTITIES OF LATTER NOT
YET KNOWN. AFTER THE SAFE WAS OPENED, SWEEZEY, TOOK FROM THE SAFE A
BOOK CONTAINING TESTIMONIALS SENT TO TESLA ON THE OCCASION OF HIS SEVEN-
TY FIFTH BIRTHDAY. THIS BOOK WAS ARRANGED FOR TESLA BY SWEEZEY.
KOSANOVICH TOOK FROM THE ROOM THREE PICTURES OF TESLA, TWO BEING EN-
LARGED NEWSPAPER PICTUREX. ACCORDING TO MANAGERS OF HOTEL AND KOSANO-
VICH HIMSELF, NOTHING ELSE WAS REMOVED FROM THE ROOM OR SAFE. THE
NOW IN POSSESSION OF KOSANOVICH. ON SATURDAY AFTERNOON, JAN
NINE, GORSUCH AND FTIZGERALD OF ALIEN PROPERTY CONTROL WENT TO
HOTEL AND SEIZED ALL THE PROPERTY OF TESLA, CONSISTING OF ABOUT TWO
TRUCKLOANDS OF MATERIAL, SEALED ALL ARTICLES AND TRANSFERRED THEM TO
THE MANHATTAN STORAGE AND WAREHOUSE CO. NY. WHERE THEY ARE NOW LOCATED.
AT THAT TIME THERE WERE ALSO IN THIS WAREHOUSE APPROXIMATELY
THIRTY BARRELS AND BUNDLES BELONGING TO TESLA WHICH HAD BEEN THERE SINCE
ABOUT NINETEEN THIRTY FOUR. THESE HAVE ALSO BEEN SEALED AND
ARE NOW UNDER ORDERS OF ALIEN PROPERTY CUSTODIAN. IN VIEW OF FACT TESLA
IS A US NATURALIZED CITIZEN, ALIEN PROPERTY CUSTODIAN FEELS THAT ITS
JURISDICTION OVER PROPERTY IS DOUBTFUL BUT FEELS THAT NO OTHER
AGENCY WILL BE ABLE TO GET TO THIS PROPERTY FOR AT LEAST TWO DAYS.
COPIES DESTROYED

REDACTIONS ON THIS PAGE ARE
NOT FOIA DELETIONS

Declassified FBI document detailing how after Tesla's death, his property
was seized by the Office of Alien Property and transferred to the
Manhattan Storage and Warehouse CO. NY.

Authentic Tesla Purple Energy Plates

WWW.TESLASECRETLAB.COM

LARGE PLATE - 12 inches X 12 inches

Because of its size, the large plate carries more energy, but, don't underestimate the power of the smaller ones! This large one is excellent for the refrigerator shelf. Under a bag of new bag groceries for a few minutes. Under a gallon of water to drink or feed plants. Plus many other uses!

Large Plate: Only $75.00 or 3 for $200 and $10.00 for shipping

SMALL PLATE - 4 - 1/2 inches X 2 - 3/4 inches

Does the same as the Large Plate above, but may be a bit easier to handle if using on a painful area. Put under your glass or bottle of water for a while, or under the sheet on your bed, in your favorite chair. There are so many uses for these versatile Plates.

Small Plate: ONLY $25.00 or 3 for $68.00 and $5.00 for shipping

PURPLE DISC - 1 - 1/2 inches in diameter

Attach to your pet's collar or under the water dish. create a necklace, put one in each shoe, carry in your purse, wallet or pocket. Easy to carry!

Purple Disc: ONLY $17.00 or 3 for $40 and $5.00 for shipping

PayPal Orders can be sent to: mrufo8@hotmail.com

Checks and money orders: Timothy Green Beckley, P.O. Box 753, New Brunswick, NJ 08903

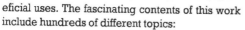

THREE CONTROVERSIAL VOLUMES

COMPLETE AND UNABRIDGED

DECODING THE LOST FORBIDDEN BOOKS OF THE HOLY BIBLE

Presented In Their Entirety— 500 Pages Of Ancient Text CENSORED By The Church!

PLUS! Available Nowhere Else! Keys To Unlocking These Rare, Nearly 2,000 Year-Old Sacred Manuscripts As Interpreted By Researcher Sean Casteel

The Books Of
ENOCH
The Books Of
JASPER
The Books Of
JUBILEES

Bible students have searched for those sacred words of scripture worthy of deep and scholarly study, but so "offensive" were they to the Church that they have been ommitted from the Holy Bible because of their controversial content. These are the books written for future generations of man whom God created after making the heavens and the earth.

Learn of The Fall; The Law; The Priesthood of Melchecizedek; Angelology; Demonology; Judgement; The Existence of the Watchers; Giants of the Earth; The Birth of Noah; The Reality of the "Ageless Ones"; The True Nature of Satan; Interpretation of Heavenly Signs and Symbols some refer to as UFOs, as well as "projections" in the sky from Godly Sources.

Go behind stained glass windows and probe the secrets of the "unorganized religion" of the Church. Includes (1) Lost Books Of The Bible; (2)Excluded Books Of The Bible; (3) Signs Of The Second Coming. **All three books just $39.00 + $6.00 S/H.**

5: And when I was asleep, great distress came up into my heart, and I was weeping with my eyes in sleep, and I could not understand what this distress was, or what would happen to me.

6: And there appeared to me two men, exceeding big, so that I never saw such on earth; their faces were shining like the sun, their eyes too were like a burning light, and from their lips was fire coming forth with clothing and singing of various kinds; in appearance purple their wings were brighter than gold, their hands whiter than snow.

7: They were standing at the head of my bed and began to call me by my name.

From *The Secrets of Enoch*

❏ **ORDER LOST—FORBIDDEN—BOOKS OF THE BIBLE**
Timothy Green Beckley · Box 753
New Brunswick, NJ 08903

For more information about Nikola Tesla, visit our website at:
www.teslasecretlab.com

Write for our free catalog at:

Global Communications
P.O. Box 753
New Brunswick, NJ 08903

Email: mrufo8@hotmail.com

Don't forget to also visit Mr. UFOs Secret Files on YouTube.

https://www.youtube.com/channel/CmaoV5iPH7kkV5CyqjybYeg

Made in the USA
Middletown, DE
31 August 2023

37739697R00046